Clouds and Sunshine

Clouds and Sunshine

Sarah Lee Brown Fleming

MINT EDITIONS

Clouds and Sunshine was first published in 1920.

This edition published by Mint Editions 2021.

ISBN 9781513283081 | E-ISBN 9781513288109

Published by Mint Editions®

MINT
EDITIONS
minteditionbooks.com

Publishing Director: Jennifer Newens
Design & Production: Rachel Lopez Metzger
Project Manager: Micaela Clark
Typesetting: Westchester Publishing Services

THIS LITTLE BOOK
I AFFECTIONATELY DEDICATE
TO MY CHILDREN,
DOROTHY AND HAROLD

Contents

Dorothea

The stars in Heaven now shine with a fuller, gladder light,
My days no longer seem a long and dreary night;
Since thou dost love me dear, all things seem more than bright,
    Dorothea, Dorothea, my own Dorothea.

If griefs and sorrows come, they do not pierce so deep,
If tears bedim my eyes they are the bitter-sweet,
If death doth part us here, I know somewhere we'll meet,
    Dorothea, Dorothea, my own Dorothea.

And e'en though death does come, I'll always see thy face,
Thy hand within my own I ever will embrace,
Remembrance of thee in my soul will have a place.
    Dorothea, Dorothea, my own Dorothea.

Tuskegee

Sacred spot on which thou art,
  O school of industry.
Thou art doing well thy part
  To aid humanity.

On thy consecrated ground
  Is carved a wondrous story,
Out of chaos, Washington
  Raised this place to glory.

The world has made a beaten track
  Unto thy very door,—
A fountain on the desert sands
  Thou art for evermore.

DEATH

The spirit out of it hath flown,
And left the body all alone,
So after all, what is this clay,
Which we so cherish, can you say?

Look on this form now still in death,
The force is gone which we call breath;
The faculties, yes, every one,
Have stopped their use, with spirit gone.

O death, thou art so grim and drear,
What awful silence thou doth wear.
And thou must visit ev'ry one,—
Yes, every being 'neath the sun.

O, death, thou art a woeful state,
All mankind well doth thee berate,—
Because we know not what awaits
Beyond thy grey, mysterious gates.

Ah death, if I could truly say,
"I fear thee neither night nor day!"
If I but knew to what estate
My wandering spirit might awake—

I would not quake when thou art near,
Thy presence I would not so fear;
But 'tis the mystery that attends
Thy awful mission, that offends.

WHEN LOVE SLEEPETH

Love built a fairy bower, with roses red and white,
And watched it ev'ry hour to keep the flowers bright:
For oh, it was so fair, this bower which love did make,—
A benediction, prayer, its perfume ever spake.

And when the chill frost came, Love showered warmth and kisses,
For whom Love doth caress, the frost he surely misses:
But one night Love did sleep, the frost was round about,
He pierced the roses deep to blot their sweetness out.

Oh, desolation drear hath gripped Love's rosy bower,
No brightness find we there, for Love hath lost all power,
Ah, Love will sometimes sleep, too oft when needed most,
And will not always keep forever at her post.

Come Let Us Be Friends

Come, let us be friends, you and I,
  E'en though the world doth hate at this hour;
Let's bask in the sunlight of a love so high
  That war cannot dim it with all its armed power.

Come, let us be friends, you and I,
  The world hath her surplus of hatred today;
She needeth more love, see, she droops with a sigh,
  Where her axis doth slant in the sky far away.

Come, let us be friends, you and I,
  And love each other so deep and so well,
That the world may grow steady and forward fly,
  Lest she wander towards chaos and drop into hell.

Man's Inconstancy

The earth revolves,
    The sun doth shine,
The moon at night,
    With stars divine,
All tell us that
    Fond nature's way,
Is much the same
    From day to day.

We know at night,
    When tasks are done,
We'll sleep to wake
    And greet the sun.
We know the spring
    With gentle grace,
To summer will
    Give up its place.

What man is like
    Fond nature true?
Can we depend
    On what he'll do?
Today he steps
    With heavy tread.
Tomorrow finds
    Him full of dread.

Today he'll swear
    By all the gods
You can rely
    Upon his words.
Tomorrow, he
    Will say to you,
"I did not speak
Those words untrue."

And so it is,
   From day to day,
We can't depend
   On what men say.
All thro' our lives
   We'll meet but few
Whom we can trust,
   Whose hearts beat true.

COMFORT

I take my cares to Jesus,
    And lay them at His feet.
He will for every sorrow
    Give consolation sweet.

Upon my head He places
    His hand so tenderly,
He tells me that He giveth
    His love to comfort me.

Oh Christ, Oh Benediction,
    Where could I go for rest,
But here upon thy foot-stool,
    Or else upon thy breast?

Dear Savior, I do feel thee
    Forever at my side;
Take not from me thy presence,
    But with me e'er abide.

The Spirit of a Friend

Back to the dust went the dust of the body,
    But the spirit that turned to its Maker on high,
Filled the air, as it passed, with so wistful a sweetness,
    That its fragrance will linger through years that slip by.

My Fortune

A gypsy wandered by one day,
When I was young and blithe and gay,
She begged me in a way so free,—
"Come, have your fortune told by me."

Now certainly, if we could chance,
To know our future in advance,
Would we not think the matter o'er,
Before the gypsy left our door?

Well, this I did, in days before
Experience had taught me; Lo,
I told her I would pay her well,
If she my future life would tell.

I sat me down, and so did she,
My hand she took upon her knee;
"Ah, Miss," said she, "will you but hear,
These rings you have shall cost you dear."

The precious rings I treasured so,
A mother's gift, if you must know.
I said "If these I should not wear
I'll take them off and hold them dear."

"Ah, no," she said, "that will not do";
"I'll hold them for a blessing, true,
And when I give them back again,
The world can ne'er more cause thee pain."

"Gypsy," I said, "I cannot part
With these dear rings so near my heart,
A mother's gift I must retain,
Gypsy, you plead for these in vain!"

She said, "If you'll not give them o'er,
Ill luck I see for you in store,
Circles around thee do revolve,
In blackness they will thee involve!"

"Give o'er thy rings and thou shalt see
Thy bondage turned to liberty,
Riches and love and fame are thine,
Circles so bright do thee enshrine!"

Her eye was set upon my gold.
Plotting for it her heart was cold;
No sentiment could change her aim,
Her blood was up, for gold she came.

Forgive me, friends, when this I say,
I forthwith gave those rings away.
I truly thought she had the power
To change my fortune in that hour.

I've lived to learn since that sad day,
That none can know—whate'er you pay,
Your fortune lies twixt God and you
Who says he knows, he speaks untrue.

The Witch

Lo, the witch all shriveled and old!
Come in and have your fortune told.
She, by the aid of a magic wand,
Can see the future in your hand.
What in your hand she cannot trace,
She'll surely find it in your face.
She'll tell you when you're going to wed,—
If the friend long gone is alive or dead.
If you'll be poor or you'll have gold,
Come in and have your fortune told!

SARAH LEE BROWN FLEMING

PAL, LET'S BE TRUE

Pal, let's be true,
I will, will you?
Our country calls to the strife.
Come to its aid,
Don't be afraid,—
For it to save, what's a life?

Yes, we will go,
Fighting? Ah more,—
We'll never know a retreat.
Proudly we move,
And e'en will prove,
Our fight the best in the feat.

Wonderful land,
Think of the hand
America takes in the fight.
Hers is to brave,
Hers is to save,
For justice, truth and the right.

A Nibbling Mouse

The swiftest, nibbling, little mouse,
Has made its home within my house,
I set a trap both night and day,
To try and catch it if I may,—
    This nibbling, little mouse.

Today when writing at my desk,
Out it came to make a quest.
It ran around with so much glee,
Seemed not a bit afraid of me,—
    This nibbling, little mouse.

Straightway I rose and got my broom
To chase the creature from the room.
Round and round it scampered fast;
Trying to catch, I darted past
    This nibbling, little mouse.

We kept the chase up half an hour,
Until I felt I'd lost all power
To chase behind it any more,
So left it prattling on the floor,—
    This nibbling, little mouse.

All tired out, I then sat down
And soon within a study, brown,
I thought of phantoms, as they pass,
And how thro' life we chase them as
    This nibbling, little mouse.

Yes, all thro' life we find it so,—
Chasing shadows as we go,
We almost catch them, but alas,
They baffle us and slip on, as
    This nibbling, little mouse.

BOY AT SCHOOL IN ENGLAND

Mother, could you but know
    What thoughts I have of thee,
Your little boy so far away,
    In this land across the sea.

Mother, could you but look
    Within my eyes so wet
With tears, because I miss you so,—
    This yearning I regret.

Could you but listen as I talk
    Of love and home and you;
My heart so fills I cannot keep
    The grief from coming through.

Last night I dreamed I felt
    Your kiss upon my cheek.
And thought I could not live without
    That touch another week.

The boys around have mothers
    Who see them off and on.
Sometimes I feel so lonesome,
    As if mine were dead and gone.

Oh, Mother, it is awful when
    A boy can't have the treat
To see his mother now and then.
    Such luck, it can't be beat.

Say, Mother, won't you promise
    When the next big ship sets sail,
You'll come yourself upon it,
    Instead of sending mail?

What Is It?

There is a subtle something
    That speaks where'er you go,
By tongue it is not uttered,
    Than words it speaks much more.

You go forth on your missions,
    And carry it along;
It's like some beauteous flower,
    And like some soothing song.

It's like some fragrant perfume
    That's wafted by the breeze.
It gives out so much comfort
    It sheds abroad such ease.

What is this subtle something?
    Folks ask me, and I say
I cannot well define it
    Nor either teach the way.

It is an inner something.
    I know that it must be
Clear shining through your body
    And giving light to me.

I love to have you near me.
    Just why I cannot say,
But this I know, your presence
    Just changes night to day.

Methought I saw a halo
    Surrounding your fair form,
When you approached that mother
    Whom death had left forlorn.

And then when asked for service,
    As fleetful as a bird,
You answered with a presence
    Which spoke far more than word.

I would, if you would charge me,
    Perform some duty true,
That I may ever daily
    Grow more like unto you.

What is that subtle something
    You carry where you go?
I long to have you name it
    Oh do, that I may know.

DIALECT POEMS

Mammy

Large of frame, black of face,
Spotless apron 'round her waist,
Teeth so pearly, eyes so true,
Make you think of heav'n so blue,
    That's Mammy.

Moving 'round the house with ease,
Trying ev'ryone to please.
In and out with so much grace,
Acting like she owned the place,
    That's Mammy.

Sister trudging down the hall
Trips o'er rug and has a fall,
Quick as lightning Mammy's there
Fussing with the hurt and scare.
    Dear Mammy.

Jane has fallen in the dirt.
Soiled all her nice new skirt,
Comes a-cryin' to the place;
Stops soon as she sees the face
    Of Mammy.

Mammy soothes the hurt and scare
Till there's none left anywhere,
With her "Hush, now Honey, do!
Mammy loves you through and through."
    Oh Mammy!

Mammy now has passed away,
But the memory lives today
With me, and shall never die,
Though the years go flitting by.
    Blest Mammy.

DE TANGO LESSON

Start up de ban'!
De men folks stan'
And take yo' partners for dis
    tango-flam.

Now step right so,—
Light on de flo',
    Forward,—an' now backward
        you all mus' go.

Don' step so hard,
O, bless de Lord!
See Jim done slip like
    de flo' is lard.

Now start again,
I makes it plain,
Forward an' backward
    den ben' yo' frame—

Now do it once mo',
Den I'll say go,—
And' keep up dat move-
    ment all roun' de flo'.

Miss Nancy Jane,
Ketch up yo' train!
It mus'n't be a-draggin';
    Does I speak plain?

Look at dem feet,
See how they meet,
No regiment of soldiers
    is got dem beat.

Now ain't dat gran,
Jus' watch Jack Ran,
He's leadin' dem dancers
    like a soldier man!

Look at ole Pop,
Jus' like a top,
I ain't seed him move
    from dat one spot!

Watch sister Cloe,
How she do go,
A-swingin' an' a-swayin'
    jus' watch her on de flo'!

Watch Ephraim's pace,
Now ain't dat grace?
Lor' help me, dese darkies
    is jus' eatin' up de place!

Just' watch dat time,
How dey keeps in line;
Lor' help me, dis music
    and dis dancin' is divine!

Ah, let 'er go!
Hear dat music flow,
Dey's playin' dis tango,
    like dey ain't no mo!

Look at ole Pop!
Make dat music stop.
He's dancin' like de devil
    done nail him to dat spot!

Here, clear de flo',
Sam, ope' de do'.
We ain't gwine to dance
    dis tango any mo'.

BACK-SLIDING LIZA

What's dat Honey, you jis say,
World ain't 'ligious in dis day?
Bless my soul, jis' know dat's so?
I done knowed dat long ago.
Lord dis world does move so fas',
'Ligion now's a thing o' the pas';
Wonder what's the end to be,
I don' know an' I can't see.
All I know I'm satisfied,
Lord I's stickin' on your side.
Dere's my gal,—Liza Jane,
Lordy me, dat gal is vain,
All she thinks about is style.
Lord, dat gal'll drive me wil'.
Talk about your edication,
Lize kin read thro' Revelation,
But her 'ligion's been neglected.
Lize's soul has ne'er been 'fected.
Honey, don't you know dese schools
Never had no kind of rules.
All my money gone to waste
Lize can't pray now, lost de tas'.
What I gwine to do, Miss Ca'line,
Wid dat wayward gal o' mine.
Pray an' it will be alright?
Well, I prays both day an' night,—
Lord, do take dis gal o' mine,
In dose mighty hands o' thine.
Shut her eyes to all dis show,—
So invitin' here below.
Show her Lord, de perfec' way,
I done foun' dis many a day.
When she, Lord, Thy love confes'
Shiel' her, Father, on Thy breas'.

The Lonesome Man

Little Rassus Wickens, sittin' in de do',
Mammy's gone to market, hear him cryin' low,
"Mammy why'd you go an' lef me all a-lone,
I's yo' little Honey, Mammy, come back home."

All de odder chil'n playin in de san'
But dis little darkey is one lonesome man,—
Listen to dose heart-throbs as he cries so low,
Little Rassus Wickens, sittin' in de do'.

Ah, within dat chile-breas', chile of darkes' hue,—
Mother love is dyed in royal color too,
Listen to dose heart-throbs, as he cries so low,
Little Rassus Wickens, sittin' in de do'.

RACE POEMS

THE BLACK MAN'S PLEA

Chains of bondage did imprint,
Far deeper wounds than one could see.
Sinking through flesh and blood and bone,
They struck the deeper life that is
Beneath the flesh, wherein doth course
The blood that carnal life doth give.
Their piercing darts did wound the life,
That's more than carnal in the man.
Stag'ring underneath the blow,
Which quelled a life-blood for a while,
And which today hath not regained
Its former circulation.   Life-blood
That doth make men, men!   Not the
Corpuscles of red and white that
Coursing through veins do lend them hue,
But, life-blood that doth give that force
Which makes a glorious race of men,
And fills with pride and all things true,
Giving an everlasting hope!

Prostrate he lay upon his back
Till freedom nursed him back again
To perfect health?—Ah, far from that,
'Tis long 'ere that can be enjoyed.
The race, still crippled by the blow
Is like a tree supposed dead,—
Showing now and then some signs of life.
Mankind! no blow is great as that
Which strikes through flesh and blood and bone,
And wounds the vital parts where lives
The greater, nobler life of man.

Ye who look without today,
Upon a race of tardy men,
Whose step is lax and spirit slow;
Although they measure not with those

Who, generations freed, have built
What liberty alone can raise,
Great monuments,—that do proclaim
Much credit to their mighty minds,
Forbearance, do I ask of you.

And do not chide this crippled race
That, convalescent, tries to stand
But totters still from slav'ry's blow.
Tear down your veil of prejudice,
And look ye forth with naked eye
Upon the field of wounded men.
See, some do rise above that plain
Of desolation and despair,
And still go forth with willing hands
To turn the wheels of progress too,
In spite of all that was and is.

Emancipation Celebration

Dear friends, we're gathered here tonight,
To celebrate a great birth-right;
Which came to us when Lincoln said
That bondage must be stricken dead;
Or else the country great and grand,
Would totter so it could not stand.
To him appeared in Spirit bold,
The great George Washington of old,
Said he, "This conflict cannot last,
It drains our country's life blood fast.
Haste Lincoln! set these people free,
It is not right, it must not be.

So Lincoln we all know so well,
Did set them free. Could I but tell
What shouts arose when bonds were broke,
The country trembled at the stroke
When slav'ry fell. A few remain,
The G. A. R.'s, to tell again
How on the field of fire and blood
They risked their lives, and bravely stood
To help the cause, with all their might.
Dear friends, they are our guests tonight,
Since dear old Lincoln is not here,
They are the next to him most dear.

From slavery forth, without one cent,
With spirit broke, my people went
To wander in the world so cold;
To find a place, and oft were told,
Your pedigree we cannot trace,—
You're classed with an unfavored race.
Forthwith they went with awful taint,
The nature now I will not paint;
The chattels of another race.

O God, 'twas hard to find a place.
Who says the race has not progressed?
He doth not know, we've had the test.

Despite these drawbacks ev'ry one,
We're here to tell what we have done,
And say, if some do not advance
As people do who've had the chance
Of longer years than we've been free.
Just reason why and you shall see.
See what we've done in fifty years!
Another fifty are my prayers
The man unborn will yet perceive
A progress now we can't conceive.

He to the world will then expose,
A worthier race and how it rose.
We've gone part way and I discern
The light of hope as it doth burn.
Plod on, my race, to reach the goal;
The path is rough, but that's the toll.
Plod on, to get with all our might,
The things we ought with our birthright!

Radiant Woman

I passed among the lowly poor,
    Within a little street,
A mother sat within her door,
    A baby at her feet.

In speaking of that mother,
    I cannot say that she
Had pedigree behind her,
    The same as you, or me.

For she was bound in body,
    (As some are wont to say).
Her race, not very lofty,
    Was being crushed that day.

'Tis sad it is the custom,
    In this enlightened time,
That people, not in wisdom,
    Are prone to draw a line,—

And say that human creatures,
    Because their skin is black,
Because they've ugly features,
    Must all be pushed right back.

This mother as she sat there,
    Did open up to me,
A realm, so full of grandeur,
    From darkness, oh, so free!

Her face though in its blackness,
    Was radiant as the sun,
Her features, plain and homely,
    Seemed glorious ev'ry one.

What was this revelation,
    I asked myself that day?
That wondrous penetration,
    That to my soul made way?

O yes, 'twas more than human.
    I must in truth admit.
I saw more than the woman
    Who in the door did sit.

I saw that inward something
    A-calling out to me,—
"Look you beyond the body,
    Divinity you'll see!"

The look that was so glorious,
    Transplanted on that face,
Told me a Christ victorious,
    Had in her heart found place.

The Dying Negro

Seems to me in lookin' over yonder,
    I see the day a-growin' very dark,
Seems to me while in dis' lan' I wander,
    No joyful song is heard from singin' lark.

Seems to me some lonesome note is stealin',
    O'er barren waste, from achin' people's souls.
Seems to me I hear some lips repeatin'
    "That sorrow in dis' lan' like waves do roll."

Seems to me I hear some distant voices
    Echoin' forth from slav'ry times to me
Seems to me they ask me what I sigh for
    And tells me to be happy 'cause I'm free.

Seems to me I answer an' I tells them
    That slav'ry's chains are broken off my han's,
Seems to me those very chains are bindin'
    My soul so close and closer with their ban's!

Seems to me I hear my people sighin',
    For help, God's help, in dis ungrateful lan',
Seems to me I hear my people cryin'
    "These burdens Lord are more than we can stan'."

Seems to me the freedom that we cherished
    Is bein' robbed from out our very lives,
Seems to me that which we thought had perished
    Is growin' now to one enormous size.

Seems to me I hear some holy voices,
    A-chantin' now some heav'nly song to me,
Seems to me my soul within rejoices,
    For death at las' has come to make me free!

THE BLACK MAN'S HOPE

I hear the talk of the white man's hope
    In the ring and at the poll,
But never a word of the black man's hope
    Do I hear as time doth roll.

Bowed with the weight which slavery left
    Upon his chattled frame,
No star of hope comes into view
    The weight is still the same.

O prejudice, cursed prejudice,
    'Tis thou that blights the way,
And makes us feel there is no hope
    There is no fairer day.

Thou poisoned venom, prejudice,
    Who gavest thee thy birth?
Art born of devil or of man,
    How camest thou on earth?

I've heard it said that some believe,
    That God so in his love
Ordained that man be bound to man,
    Do you believe the above?

Do you believe such laws are made
    That blacks should till the soil,
While other races reign supreme,
    Removed from all such toil?

Why, God created all men here
    Upon one level plane.
All bodies of the dust were made,
    To dust must go again.

Then why should color play such part
    Upon this mortal earth?
No man has power to change his skin,
    WE'RE ACCIDENTS OF BIRTH.

An Exhortation

Is there no prophet, seer nor bard,
    At this compelling time,
To sing a song or say a word,
    Or even write a line?
Is there an ear that will not hear,
    The wails, the groans of men,
Of suckling infants, babes unborn,
    Oh, who will ease their pain?

Is there a mouth that will not speak,
    Of wrongs they do endure,
No tongues that in a language may
    Some remedy outpour?
Speak, oh, ye long dumb mouths, oh speak,
    And to a people tell
The burden forced upon you now
    Makes earth to you a hell.

A battle fierce is raging,
    Unlike the usual fray,
'Tis worse than other conflicts
    That are fought by night or day.
Those men at last find succor,
    The helpless blind and lame,
But none comes to that woeful depth,—
    The heart, when full of pain.

This pain's an awful burden,
    To trudge on day by day.
It crushes soul and body
    And makes indifference play;
It shoots right to the marrow
    Of life, its hopes, and oh,
Threatens the very right to live,
    Tries manhood to o'erthrow.

O bards, who in the days of yore,
    Did move a nation's heart,
Who with your great and glorious strain
    Did still a turbulent mart,
Come sing again another strain
    Of duty, and above
All else, oh, sing that glorious strain,—
    That wondrous strain of love.

Sing them a wondrous story
    This burdened race of men,
Paint it with all the glory that
    Can come forth from your pen.
Set it to tuneful melody,
    As ever man did hear,
So that a race benighted
    Will sing with heartiest cheer.

Pictures

I. Slavery

Gaze on this picture of the past,
 See cruel master, whip in hand,
 Upon yon slave, whose back is bent,
 Scourge upon scourge he letteth fall.
"My God, my God!" the slave doth cry,
"How long shall I these burdens bear?"
"To work, to work," the master cries,
"Go fill my coffers with thy brawn."
Who doth not know, who hath not felt,
 For those who lived in that sad time?
What is the life of him who slaves,
 Whose body is not called his own?
They bore the stripes, endured the pain,
 With not one murmur but to pray.
They sang the songs we all do know,
 The songs that we shall sing again.
These prayers and songs were wafted up,
 And, oh, they were so wondrous sweet,
They reached a throne where sits a Judge
 Who judgeth slow but judgeth well.
They listened and they heard response—
 "I will repay, I will repay!"

II. War

Then discord rose twixt North and South,
 'Twas over slaves, you know it well.
 Came Ab'ram Lincoln to the front,
 A bloody battle to pursue.
See war in all its dreadful state,—
 A scourge of men these battles are:
 A price was paid so dear in blood,
 By North and South in that great war,
 That not a home was left without

Some loved one gone forevermore.
A cry was made for volunteers
Who'll answer it? Ah, you can tell.
See black men marching to the front,
With steady step and wondrous stride,
How fearlessly they go to die!
And yet they say we are afraid
To risk our lives for a great cause.
Yet I believe that you or I
If needed at some future time,
Will march as proudly to the front
As they did then in sixty-three.

III. Freedom

The war is o'er, the slaves are free,
They walk abroad as man with man.
But note the frown upon the brow
Of yonder man whose skin is fair.
"I will not walk, as man with man,
With yonder black," I hear him say,
"He was not made to cope with me,
Who rule this land, whose skin is fair."
Then what is this I see unearthed,
So soon as slavery's debt is paid?
'Tis prejudice, cursed prejudice,
Another form of slavery.

IV. Lynching

See yonder mob, full fifty strong,
Hound that poor lad of Negro blood.
He fleeth to the woods, and oh,
They set the dogs upon his trail.
At last he's caught, and lo, what then?
They string him to yon leafless tree,
And to his clothes they put a flame,
And now he's in eternity.

V. Discrimination

Not wanted here, not wanted there,
Such signs go up all o'er the land.
My God, then are my people free!
No vote for you, no vote for me.
Have we not borne the stripes enough,
Our cry goes up,—"How long, how long!"

VI. Future

Let's leave these pictures of the past,
And pictures of the present time,
And wander on and on and on,
Unto some great approaching dawn.
My final picture is this one,
'Tis not with master, whip in hand,
But it is Black and White, alike,
Holding aloft the stars and stripes.
They've buried far beneath the sod
Grim prejudice and all lynch laws,
And all in one united band,
Proclaim the freedom of the land.
List, up to heaven there goes a sigh
Of long restraint, and then a cry,—
"Praise God we're free, at last we're free."

Night Song

(NEGRO LULLABY)

I.

Honey, take yo' res, on yo' Mammy's breas',
See dat light a-fadin' 'mong de pine trees in de wes'.
Yes, de day is gone, night is comin' on,
Darksome night mus' come to us before another dawn.

Chorus

Whippo-will is callin', callin' to his mate,
Mockin'-bird is callin' too,
Pine trees is a-sighin', babies is a-cryin',
As the dark-some night is passin' through.
    Go to sleep, ma little honey, go to sleep,
    Shut yo' weary eyelid an' don' you weep,
        Sleep and take yo' res',
        On yo' Mammy's breas',
    Night can never harm you here.

II.

Honey, don' you see, dat it's got to be,
Day an' night, yes, day an' night, until yo' spirit's free,
Den you'll quit ma breas', fer to go an' res'
Wid Anodder, who can pro-tec' you from harm de bes'!

Put Away That Ukelele and Bring Out the Old Banjo

I.

Don't you hear old Orpheus calling to you, Alexander Poe?
He says just quit that ukelele and play on the old banjo,
Those Honolulu jingles like the dog has had its day,
Go put the faithful banjo down, put the ukelele away.
    Chorus:
Way down upon the,—I'm coming, yes, I hear that music, oh,
Put away that ukelele man, and play on the old banjo.

2.

Put away that ukelele, bring me down the old banjo,
Sing again for me the tunes I love, Swanee River and Old Black Joe,
Then play for me those melodies my mother used to hum,
That between each syncopating note, the banjo went "Tum, tum."
    Chorus: Way down upon the, etc.

A Note About the Author

Sarah Lee Brown Fleming (1876–1963) was an African American poet, novelist, educator, and activist. Born in Charleston, South Carolina, Fleming was raised in Brooklyn, where she would become the school system's first Black teacher. In 1902, she married Richard Stedman Fleming, a pioneering African American dentist with whom she would raise a son and a daughter. In addition to her work as a teacher, Fleming was a founder of the New Haven's Women's Civic League and the Phillis Wheatley Home for Girls. A lifelong advocate for Black girls and women, she received honors and awards from the United States Congress and the National Association of Negro Business and Professional Women's Club. She also published works of literature, including *Hope's Highway: A Novel* (1918) and *Clouds and Sunshine* (1920), a collection of poems.

A Note from the Publisher

Spanning many genres, from non-fiction essays to literature classics to children's books and lyric poetry, Mint Edition books showcase the master works of our time in a modern new package. The text is freshly typeset, is clean and easy to read, and features a new note about the author in each volume. Many books also include exclusive new introductory material. Every book boasts a striking new cover, which makes it as appropriate for collecting as it is for gift giving. Mint Edition books are only printed when a reader orders them, so natural resources are not wasted. We're proud that our books are never manufactured in excess and exist only in the exact quantity they need to be read and enjoyed.

bookfinity™

Discover more of your favorite classics with Bookfinity™.

- Track your reading with custom book lists.
- Get great book recommendations for your personalized Reader Type.
- Add reviews for your favorite books.
- AND MUCH MORE!

Visit **bookfinity.com** and take the fun Reader Type quiz to get started.

Enjoy our classic and modern companion pairings!

Classic & Modern